MINDFULNESS — A DIFFERENT PLATFORM

Mind the Gap

Eleanor Gibson

Grosvenor House Publishing Limited

This book is published by
Grosvenor House Publishing Ltd
Link House
140 The Broadway, Tolworth, Surrey, KT6 7HT.
www.grosvenorhousepublishing.co.uk

A CIP record for this book
is available from the British Library

Paperback ISBN 978-1-83615-451-8
Hardback ISBN 978-1-83615-452-5
eBook ISBN 978-1-83615-453-2

Contents

Preface

Mindfulness – A Different Platform is a motivational book which follows *Mindfulness the Journey, Not the Destination* by Eleanor Gibson.

Many of our challenges in life are not of our own making and are due to the actions of other people. The relationships we have with others can impact on our mental health, quality of life and bring us deep emotional pain and anguish. Mindfulness provides the opportunity for us to pause, breathe and view our life from an entirely different platform.

These interpersonal relationships can cause us to become unbalanced and can, on occasion, hinder us from moving forward and achieving our full potential. They can make our clarity of thinking become cloudy and murky, which can lead us into deep ruts which we struggle to climb out of.

Mindfulness – A Different Platform will instil in us a sense of purpose, providing the strength and clear thinking we require to spring us into action and live our best life possible where mindfulness, compassion and gratitude are central to our way of being.

Dedication

I would like to dedicate this book to my lovely sister, Moira, and her wonderful husband, Anthony, who together have battled so bravely with cancer.

They are my inspiration to keep going and to face life with strength and commitment in helping others who may also be suffering.

I am very proud of their bravery and resilience.

Nietzsche's view:

> *'He who has a* why *to live for can bear with almost any* how*'* (cited by Frankl, 2004, p.84).

Introduction

Without Wings

I used to be a butterfly
With wings so free and bright
Flying high from plant to flower
In the morning light.

Basking in the sunshine
And soaking up the rays,
Giving me the energy
To soar on high each day.

But now I am a caterpillar
Crawling on the ground.
Wriggling bare from leaf to leaf
Waiting to be found.

My vibrant colours faded,
My wings all torn apart.
The sky is so unreachable
The flowers only art.

But soon I will be flying
And floating on the air
With oh such graceful movement
The crowds will stop and stare.

For no one can destroy me
As I have inner strength
To bring to every moment
An inner confidence.

So, watch this lovely butterfly
And never think to kill her
For this, oh so gorgeous creature,
Was once a caterpillar.

by Eleanor Gibson

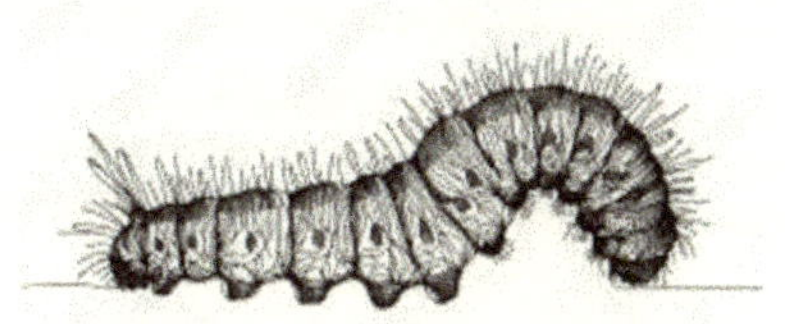

In the wise words of Antoine de Saint-Exupéry:

> '*One must endure the caterpillars if one is to become acquainted with the butterflies*' (cited by Black, 2018, p.77).

When I reflect on my life, I realise that I have not always learnt from the past. For years I kept making the same mistakes and taking the same routes, ending up back where I started. It's like going to the railway station and taking the same train, only to arrive at the same destination. Mindfulness has provided me with the clarity of vision to recognise that I have a choice. I have realised that I can go to another platform and board a different train which will take me on a new, inspiring and exciting journey.

Denis Waitley provides us with sound advice:

> *'Learn from the past, set vivid detailed goals for the future, and live in the only moment of time over which you have any control: now'* (Denis Waitley).

Chapter 1
The Mind

Random Memories

Through my mindfulness practise, I am now more aware of where my mind wanders. It never fails to amaze me the memories that pop up out of the blue. The only way that I can describe it, is like a digital photo frame, set at random, where the pictures have no order or sequence.

Childhood Memories

I remember:

- The time, on returning home from Brownies, when my sister, Moira, grabbed the budgie's tail and the budgie flew off without it.
- The night the canvas sides of Dad's lorry blew open and breadboards flew out during a hurricane, giving the elderly neighbour downstairs palpitations, as she had been busy reading a ghost story at the time.
- The night I stayed overnight at Aunt Ina's house and asked her if she wore her glasses to bed. 'Of course I do!' she replied. 'How could I possibly be able to see what I am dreaming about?' I think I was 18 before I realised that this was not, in fact, true.
- The morning that one of the boys in my Primary 3 class turned up late and the teacher asking him where he had been. When

he replied, 'Nowhere, Miss.' She promptly pulled down the classroom map of the world, handed him the pointer and demanded that he show her where 'nowhere' was.

Happy Memories

My mind can then jump to more recent memories that make me smile, such as:

- The time we took the car to a car wash in the south of France and the absolute confusion, bewilderment, astonishment and hilarity encountered in the garage remain with me to this day. My husband, who does not speak or comprehend the French language, didn't read the instructions which clearly stated that the handheld device must be held before inserting the payment. He then spent five agonising minutes chasing the wriggling wand, which was now performing like a boa constrictor on acid, all around the forecourt, much to the amusement of the French motorists. 'Mon Dieu! Les anglais sont très stupides!'
- The evening I recognised one of the superintendents from the police on the news and told my daughter that I knew him. My daughter, aged eight at the time, asked why I was calling him a 'Super Nintendo' and asked if it was because he was a 'Gameboy'.
- The afternoon I was working at Hamilton Grammar School, when the headteacher inquired about my daughter's pet rabbit. I explained that I had taken the rabbit to the vet because she kept pulling her hair out and making a nest. The vet's diagnosis was 'a phantom pregnancy'. Five minutes later, one of the clerical staff returned from the Hope Street building of the school. When the headteacher asked how she had coped at the Annexe building, she promptly replied that she had been rushed off her feet and had been pulling her hair out all morning. 'Oh dear,' he sighed, 'I hope you are not having a phantom pregnancy like Eleanor's daughter's rabbit.' Needless to say, the said member of staff looked totally bewildered and confused.

- The time my daughter, at ten years old, asking me why I hadn't married Paul McCartney. I simply advised her that he hadn't asked me to marry him. The fact that I had never even met Paul McCartney didn't seem to enter the mind of a ten-year-old.
- The day my friend Irene and I met on the train at Motherwell to travel to a road safety meeting in Edinburgh. We talked the entire journey, hardly stopping to take a breath. By the time we reached Edinburgh, we had put the world to rights and felt quite satisfied with our ramblings. It wasn't until we stood up to leave the train, and noticed the disgusted looks of the other passengers, that we realised that we had been travelling on the 'quiet carriage' where talking was not to be encouraged – oops!

Embarrassing Memories

My mind can then wander off and recall the memories that truly make me cringe:

- The afternoon that I went to the dentist after school to have my brace adjusted and the look of disbelief, horror and dismay on the dentist's face when I removed the brace from my mouth covered in bright pink bubble gum.
- The day I took part in the swimming gala at Motherwell baths. The race I entered was the pyjama race. The aim was to swim a breadth of the pool, put on your nightwear and swim back across the pool. How hard could that be? However, the rascals in my year had tied the top of my drawstring nightie tightly into a knot. Therefore, when I attempted to put it on, there was no place for my head to go. The race had finished and been applauded, and members of the audience were now in an uproar at the commotion, confusion and embarrassment I found myself in – a bright orange bri-nylon nightie, wriggling at the side of the pool like a psychedelic satsuma, frantically trying to escape from its skin.

- The piano exam in Glasgow where I was so nervous and confused at the end of the test that I inadvertently entered the broom cupboard instead of the exit door in a desperate attempt to escape from the room. The look on the examiner's face as he nervously attempted to rescue me from the array of brushes, dusters and cleaning materials, still haunts me to this day.

High School Memories

My mind can then wander to high school days and the recollection of:

- The Greek mythology lesson when the pranksters in my class smuggled in a ghetto blaster and pressed the play button each time the teacher turned towards the blackboard. When he asked who was making all the noise the boys replied that it was David Bowie. 'Right, David Bowie, come out to the front of the class now!' he ordered. Needless to say, the entire class was now in a riot, as chaos reigned.
- The first-year art class when we were asked to bring an empty wine bottle to be painted. When I asked Mum for an empty wine bottle she shrugged and gave me an alternative. The roars of laughter from my classmates are still vivid to this day, as I placed the empty milk bottle on the desk. The teacher could not contain her laughter either. How humiliating!

Recent Memories

My mind can then wander to more recent events such as:

- The Hogmanay dinner dance at the Glynhill Hotel, near Paisley, where I could smell a strong smell of burning as I sat at the dinner table. When I glanced down at the table I could see the menu going up in flames as my absent-minded husband had foolishly placed it on top of the lit tealight. It was a bit like watching the opening scene of the cowboy series, *Bonanza.*

My husband hurriedly picked up the menu, threw it to the floor and stamped out the flames with his feet. When the waitress returned to take the order, she snapped up the menu and stared at me suspiciously through the chargrilled hole in the middle, as she nervously wrote down our order.

- The day my mother-in-law informed me that she had phoned my work only to be told that I was on a training course. 'How long have you been doing that job, Eleanor?' she asked.

  'About 15 years,' I replied.

  'Well, you would think that you would have got the hang of it by now, without having to go on a training course! Does your boss go on courses?' she asked.

  'Yes,' I replied.

  'Well, he can't be up to much either!' she stated in disbelief and astonishment.

- The morning my husband was busily making porridge in the kitchen and walked calmly into the lounge and asked me if he was on fire. 'No,' I replied. (*What a strange question to ask,* I thought.) However, when he turned around to walk back into the kitchen, I could see flames going up the back of his dressing gown. I started to scream, 'You're on fire! You're on fire!'

  He walked back into the lounge and calmly said, 'I'm either on fire or I'm not on fire, make up your mind.'

  'You're on fire!' I screamed.

  He slowly removed his dressing gown, threw it onto the kitchen floor and stamped out the flames, and continued to stir the porridge. There are times in life when you just lose your appetite completely. This was indeed one of those times!

Memories can be sparked off by a sound, a smell, an image, a place, a song, a taste or even the weather or the temperature. It is worth noting that research carried out in 2024 shows that memories are not only held in the brain but can also exist in other cells within the body [Kukushkin, Carney, Tabassum, Carew, 2024].

Mood Congruent Memory

Recent research on mood-congruent memory, reveals that we are more likely to retrieve memories congruent with our present mood states (Faul and LaBar, 2023). Their findings suggest that if we are feeling sad, we are more likely to retrieve sad memories. When we are feeling angry, we are more likely to retrieve angry memories. Therefore, when we feel happy, happy memories occur. Consequently, it makes sense to invest in our own happiness and realise what actually makes us happy.

The Dalai Lama's view:

> *'I believe that the very purpose of our life is to seek happiness'* (cited by Wallace, 2007, p.3).

Once we start to practise mindfulness, we realise what actually makes us feel happy and recognise that it is the basic things in life that make us smile.

Through our mindfulness practise, we begin to recognise what mood states we are in. We are then able to establish any triggers or root causes. I have now become more aware of my mood states and triggers through practising mindfulness, and now make a conscious effort to tune in with my feelings and emotions.

> *'Brain research has revealed that finding words for feelings deactivates the part of the brain that initiates a stress response'* (Germer, 2009, p.71).

Mindfulness Practice – RAIN Practice

The following mindfulness practise helps us to **Recognise** what moods, mind states, feelings and emotions are present for us. It **Allows** us to accept our present mood and **Investigate** where we are holding or experiencing it within the body. It enables us to have an open relationship with our moods and not become them, through a process of **Non-identification.**

RAIN mindfulness meditation practice – **Appendix A**

Also available as a podcast at https://youtube.com/@eleanor-mindfulness

Chapter 2

Destructive Relationships

'Wisdom is the art of living happily. Much of that art comes from seeing how we live unhappily' (Rosenberg and Guy, 1998, p.132).

My Sandcastle

I wrote my name upon the shore,
The tide came in, my name, no more.
The grains all re-arranged, contorted,
The letters had become distorted.

I built a castle made of sand
With turrets, drawbridge, flags – how grand!
I stood and cherished my creation
I'd worked so hard with mindful patience.

I cared for it, to make it last,
Maintaining walls, all crumbling fast.
But then the waves came crashing down,
They came so fast; I feared I'd drown.

They wiped away my lovely treasure
Leaving nothing left to pleasure.
Only memories of its structure
And the time it took to nurture.

by Eleanor Gibson

The main lesson I have learnt from my experiences in life is that if you don't make a concerted effort to keep yourself mentally and physically healthy, then you could lose everything that you have built in your life so far. Destructive relationships can seriously damage your health, if you are not careful.

Being Acquainted

You can be acquainted with someone for years before you discover something about them that you didn't know. This can be simple things like going to the gym and meeting the same person each week and then finding out that their passion is panning for gold, beekeeping, bungee jumping or trainspotting. You may struggle to visualise this person in this other role, instead of the Lycra-clad person you have become accustomed to.

> *'Every day we put on different hats depending on who we are relating to'* (Chopra, 2020, p.14).

However, when you have spent a great amount of time with someone and then realise that there is a different side to them entirely, it can be deeply unnerving. This situation can be very difficult to accept if the individual is working against your values and morals. You must try your very best to ensure that other people's actions do not turn you into something you are not. Unhealthy relationships can make you cynical, resentful and bitter.

Mindfulness helps us to rise above these destructive emotions. This gives us the empowerment to live our life in a sincere and healthy way. Instead of succumbing to another person's ill-advised ways, we can use our clarity of thought to make wise choices for our own future wellbeing.

When your life, as you knew it, has been destroyed and the rug pulled out from under you, it is very difficult to get back on track. When faced with circumstances that don't belong in your life, i.e. someone has thrown in a part of another jigsaw and you spend vast amounts of time and energy trying desperately to place it into your own life's jigsaw, try as you may, it's never going to fit.

A Different Mindset

In my opinion, we are extremely fortunate if we have a roof over our heads, clothes to wear and food to eat. Each day I am grateful for the life I have. I always think of those less fortunate who don't have a home, clothes to wear or food to eat. However, some people are of a different mind-set and in the words of Alan Watts,

> *'...try to get something 'out of life', as if it were a bank to be robbed'* (cited in Sears, 2014, p.103).

They have everything they require to have a great life. They have their health, family, friends, accommodation, food and wealth, and a huge amount of material things, but this is still not enough. They live their lives in greed and selfishness. If you are a kind, considerate and caring person you may assume that other people are of the same mind-set. WRONG!

The Weeble

The Weeble will wobble but never fall down.
The others have fallen like skittles around.
He never will falter, show any remorse,
For the heartache of others, are all of his cause.

The dominos tumble like books in a row
Each affecting the next with a heart-rocking blow.
But he is still standing, no feeling or pain,
With a smile on his face at the fallen – all slain.

by Eleanor Gibson

Some people seem to get great pleasure from wrong-doings, so long as they can get away with it. When caught red-handed, they will bat the blame back at you or to someone else.

> *'Narcissistic anger serves an important function for the narcissist: it deflects negative attention away from the self toward others, who can then be blamed for all the dark emotions being experienced'* (Neff, 2015, p.143).

They do not appear to have the ability to take responsibility for their own devious actions.

If you are the type of person who loves the energy of life, the grateful sense of being alive and put your heart and soul into everything you do, you may find it difficult to cope with someone who deliberately sets out to damage that zest, energy, gratitude and compassion. Their actions can be toxic, underhand and devious.

> *'The public hero that others admire can leave quite a trail of private hurt in his wake'* (Kabat-Zinn, 2013, p.liii).

You may be too trusting and naïve to understand what is going on behind the mask. The facade of normality they portray is so convincing and believable.

Masquerade

He looks at you with laughing eyes,
His masquerade is no surprise.
You've watched him do the same to others,
His two-faced arrogance, uncovers.

His smile is menacingly evil,
His eyes are dancing something gleeful!
His little secret, oh so playful!
To glance with ease, across the table.

His barefaced cheek is deep and cruel,
He thinks you are an utter fool
To ridicule, resent, destroy.
He uses you as though a toy.

He hates the fact that he's been shaken
On the actions he has taken.
He's the one that's doing the fighting,
Throwing insults and gas lighting.

His other life you'd find quite shocking
It would leave your whole world rocking.
You'd never think he'd be so rotten
It's like a nightmare you are caught in.

You may feel your life has perished
Gone are memories you once cherished.
A life that most, would find a dream
But things, not always, as they seem.

Now you must find the strength to prosper
In your life where good will foster.
For good will always conquer evil,
Although the situation's lethal.

by Eleanor Gibson

Intention

In my opinion, the saying *'what you don't know won't harm you'* (Pettie, 1576) is totally false.

If someone in your life is working against you, without your knowledge, the energy they are giving off is very damaging, not just for you, but also for them. You will probably have realised, through experience, that when you carry out tasks haphazardly and without positive intention, it affects not just your attitude, but also the outcome.

Lynne McTaggart states,

> *'Intention appears to be something akin to a tuning fork, causing the tuning forks of other things in the universe to resonate at the same frequency'* (cited by Brown, 2010, p.101).

I believe that actions and events carried out in a particular place change the energy, atmosphere and aura of that place.

If you have been left to pick up the pieces from a traumatic experience, it can be so debilitating and exhausting. Mindfulness can provide the opportunity to view the situation from a different perspective. Sometimes, when we are emotionally wounded, we stick a plaster over the wound and hope that things will mend themselves. What we should realise is that the wound could be poisonous, and we risk infection spreading around the body to perhaps the heart, brain or stomach.

> *'Never underestimate the role of mental, emotional and psychological factors in ill-health: toxins of the mind manifest as toxins of the body'* (Brown, 2010, p.178).

The Aftermath

The aftermath can be just as bewildering as you struggle to deal with the shock. It's the same feeling you get when a close loved one has died, and you are following the hearse to the crematorium. You are not connected to normality or reality. You are in disbelief that people can continue with their daily lives, whilst you are experiencing such devastation:

> *'Ye banks and braes o'bonnie Doon*
> *How can ye bloom sae fresh and fair?*
> *How can ye chant, ye little birds,*
> *And I sae weary, fu' o' care'*

(Burns, 1791)

Moving Forward

Recognising that they have the problem, and not you, is key to moving forward with confidence and reassurance. You can become the devastation or use it to spring into action and build on stronger foundations and perhaps help others in the process. Other people's actions can seriously affect our mental health, but:

> *'Why let the momentum of another person's agenda catapult you into a severe imbalance of body and mind just at the moment when you need all your inner resources for being clear and strong?'* (Kabat-Zinn, 2013, p.488).

It can be all too easy for us to let the devious actions of others cloud our vision and destroy our joie de vivre. This is where mindfulness can help us, by enabling us to pause, step back and regain our vantage point. Mindfulness can provide that inner strength to see things as they really are. Mindfulness lets you know that you have a choice.

I quote Martin Stepek, an inspiring mindfulness teacher, poet and author:

> *'Scottish people are generally good, but not all of the time. Polish people are generally good, but not all of the time. German people are good, but not all of the time'* (Stepek, 2024).

Martin's words of wisdom have helped me to put things into perspective and move forward and progress in my life, under very difficult circumstances.

Restoring Equilibrium

Life is challenging. When we are quite literally knocked off our perch by other people's actions, decisions or life choices, we really need to make a conscious and mindful effort to restore our equilibrium and balance the scales again in order to stay healthy.

This can be difficult if the mind and body are in a state of shock or disarray. Dr Antonovsky's view:

> '*...being healthy involves an ability to continuously restore balance in response to its continual disruption*' (cited by Kabat-Zinn, 2013, p.248).

Imagine if you went to see the Royal Scottish National Orchestra and the conductor did not turn up. The trumpets, saxophones, flutes, oboes, trombones, harps, piano and violins would all be playing at once to the wrong beat, with no definitive sound or rhythm. You would not hear the beautiful music, the crescendos or harmony, due to the loud din of noise. Therefore, it is important that we take charge of our mind. Tune it regularly, through mindfulness practise, just like you would tune a musical instrument. That way it will function smoothly, sound beautiful and sharp and be in harmony. In the words of Wolf Singer from the Max Planck Institute in Frankfurt, Germany:

> '*The brain is an orchestra without a conductor*' (cited by Germer, 2009, p.96).

Mindfulness Practice – Training the Mind to Focus

Training the Mind to Focus mindfulness meditation practice – **Appendix B**

Also available as a podcast at https://youtube.com/@eleanor-mindfulness

Chapter 3

Relationships – Please Mind the Gap

'No one in your life is with you constantly
No one is completely on your side,
And though I move my world to be with him,
Still, the gap between us is too wide.
Looking back, I could have played it differently
Learned about the man before I fell
But I was ever so much younger then
Now, at least I know, I know him well.'

(Rice, Andersson and Ulvaeus, 1986)

Losing Yourself in Others

Throughout my life, I have witnessed many people lose themselves in others. They lose their identity and become an add-on to the more powerful individual in the relationship. No matter what relationship we have with others, we still have to maintain our own beliefs, values, moral standards, personality and outlook.

In some relationships it is difficult to see where one person ends and the next begins – there is no gap. In other relationships, the gap can be so vast that the relationship hardly exists at all. In my opinion, the gap is vitally important. The right gap in any relationship enables you to grow and flourish as a unique human being, whilst being in the relationship, contributing to the rich tapestry of life.

A prime example of losing your identity, as an individual, can sometimes happen when you have children and become 'Chloe's mum' or 'David's dad'. Teachers and youth leaders may just always refer to you by your child's name. You may even feel that you are an anonymous enabler as you transport your child from one activity to another.

Minding the Gap

The following examples are a prime example of where a healthy gap has not been minded:

Jan* found herself in a relationship where her partner controlled everything – what she ate, what she wore and how her house was organised. She was not allowed to experiment with furniture or décor in her own home, which led to her losing interest in, or even attempting to improve her living space.

When in company, her partner would be the dominant one who led all conversations which resulted in Jan losing her confidence in her ability to communicate and contribute on any subject matter. When Jan began a conversation or tried to relate a story, her partner would talk over the top of her and then finish relating the story from his viewpoint.

> Jan explains: *'When we were together in company, I felt as if I was being submerged underwater, as my partner needed to be the centre of attention at all times, leaving me feeling lonely and vulnerable. I felt as if I had ceased to exist.'*

Jan discovered that mindfulness helped her see things more clearly and gave her the strength to alter her diet and to make small changes to put her stamp on things. Jan began to spend time with like-minded people from her mindfulness class, and gradually found that she too had a voice and could make positive contributions to conversations which gave her more confidence in company.

Elaine* had found herself so under pressure at work and struggling to keep on top of housework and shopping that she failed to notice how distant her partner had become. When she returned from work early one day, she discovered that her partner was leading a double life – a life that she certainly wasn't part of. Elaine struggled to come to terms with the fact that the man she had loved could be so cruel, underhand and devious. *'I felt as if I had just been the domestic help and cleaner in our home, whilst he had been living the life of Riley. How could this happen to me after all the years of working, contributing and building our lovely home?'*

Elaine, through her mindfulness practise, gained a sense of worth and spent less time doing chores and spent more time doing the things that truly lifted her spirits. She realised that, in the past, all her efforts and energy were directed at others. Through mindfulness she found her true self.

Jim* found himself in a totally intolerable situation at the hospital where he worked. He was being bullied by a female colleague. She had been criticising his work and was constantly on his case. He overheard her mimic him to other colleagues, ridiculing his mannerisms and laughing at his struggles and insecurities. *'I felt totally humiliated,'* explained Jim. *'I couldn't stop crying.'*

Jim recognised, through practising mindfulness, that he could find that inner strength to cope better with his work situation. Mindfulness provided the opportunity to realise that he was a good, hard-working, reliable employee. He found the clarity to recognise that he was not the problem and that his expertise and knowledge in his work were what mattered to him. He focused more on providing an excellent service to his patients. His kind and compassionate nature helped him to spring into action and excel in his career.

Jane* found out, quite by accident, that her son was using social media in an unhealthy way in order to gain admiration and attention from people online. Her son had been experiencing behavioural problems at school and his teachers had contacted

Jane about his bullying and narcissistic behaviour. *'He seemed to have turned into a domineering, controlling and aggressive boy overnight,'* Jane explained. *'I was worried sick.'*

Jane had come across an article about how mindfulness could perhaps help her son to develop a healthier relationship with others [Giancola, M., Perazzini, M., Bontempo, D., Perilli, E., and D'Amico, S., 2024]. She then found some online mindfulness practices for her son to listen to on a daily basis. Through mindfulness practise, Jane's son has developed a more stable relationship with her, his teachers, his classmates and his friends on social media. He doesn't experience the feelings of 'missing out' and is more able to control his emotions. A healthy gap between him and his acquaintances on social media has now been found.

Lorraine* had supported her friend continuously over the years through difficult and turbulent times. Her friend seemed to bounce from one relationship to the next, leaving a trail of destruction and chaos in her midst, resulting in Lorraine trying to help her piece her life together again. Each time her friend met a new partner, Lorraine was dropped like a hot brick, leaving a sense of loss and bewilderment. Lorraine explained, *'I felt totally abandoned, rejected and lonely. I then blamed myself for being so gullible, but I still failed to learn when to walk away. I continued to help her rebuild her life until I was too exhausted to carry on. I now feel as if part of me is missing.'*

Through her mindfulness practise, Lorraine realised that she had lost herself in the relationship by giving all her energy and support to her friend. This had depleted her own quality of life. She began to realise that she was sharing the suffering that her friend had brought upon herself. Mindfulness helped her to focus on what was important to her and to concentrate on the things in life that made her feel valued and appreciated. This resulted in her being able to take up new interests and join classes that benefitted her. Her friend then began to realise that she had to be responsible for her own actions.

May* met her partner through work. After a whirlwind romance, brief engagement and wedding, she found that her new husband didn't seem to be interested in progressing in his career and kept making excuses to leave his places of employment saying that he was unfit to work. May worked all of the hours she could to compensate for her husband's lack of earnings but couldn't meet the expenses of his lavish lifestyle. May says, *'I felt economically crippled and although I was working every hour I could, I couldn't meet the level of his outgoings, which were unnecessarily draining. I couldn't afford new clothes and struggled to buy food.'*

May, as a result of her mindfulness practise, realised that she was fortunate enough to always be employed in jobs that she enjoyed and that were suited to her personality and life skills. Through encouragement, she was able to motivate her husband to find his true calling, working in the great outdoors. It was a win/win situation for both of them.

I think sometimes it can be so easy to lose ourselves in others, especially if we have strong-willed people in our life. I think it is worth noting, however, that:

> *'Everyone deserves to be in a relationship where they feel safe, respected, and valued – and that includes you'* (Calm, 2024).

If this is not the case, you can begin to doubt yourself and experience a feeling of isolation. The situation may even lead to you not even acknowledging and respecting yourself. However, through your mindfulness practise, you will begin to realise that everything in your life should start with you. You will begin to discover the unique, authentic and genuine person that you are.

Through your mindfulness practise, you will realise that no matter the challenges you have to face, that you still have choices and that you can take every opportunity to nurture yourself and follow your dreams.

The Company we Keep

It's a true saying *'you get like the company you keep'* (Euripides). It is, therefore, important to choose your friends wisely.

I once knew a very wise lady who frequently used these sayings: *'if you fly with the crows, you get shot with the crows'* and *'stop the world, I want to get off'*. I could never quite understand what she meant by these phrases. As I have progressed through life, however, I realise exactly what she meant. The company we keep can affect our way of being and how we see the world. It also affects how people view us in the world. Sometimes we get caught up in other peoples' viewpoints and beliefs and just drift along like sheep, as this is what is expected of us. This can happen in both our personal and professional lives.

We may not even realise that we are being manipulated or brainwashed. This can quite easily happen when we are so busy leading hectic and challenging lives in an effort to juggle everything from organising our home, paying the bills, childcare and working in a stressful environment. When we are working in a hectic environment it can be a bit overwhelming, as not only are you expected to carry out the tasks designated to you, but you have to deal with all the office politics and personality traits that surround you. People's personality traits can deeply affect us and impact on how we actually function in our daily lives. Traits such as bullying can be humiliating, hurtful and intimidating and this can be at a verbal, physical or psychological level. In some cases, this can become too much to handle. In addition, many people like to download all their personal problems onto you in an effort to lighten their own load. In my opinion, a great deal of time, effort and resources are allocated to the risks and dangers of 'lone working', but not enough emphasis is given on how to work with all the different and difficult personalities on a daily basis. I remember days where I used to experience a feeling of being overpowered in my working environment.

On many occasions, I felt as if I was taking part in a play. There were so many different characters.

The ones who:

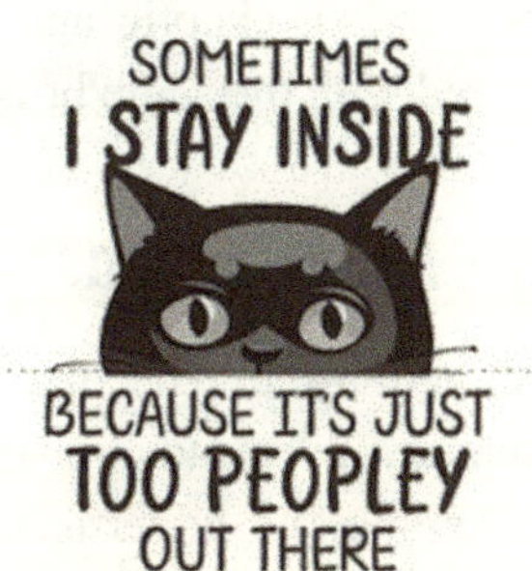

SOMETIMES
I STAY INSIDE
BECAUSE ITS JUST
TOO PEOPLEY
OUT THERE

- could charm the birds off the trees
- thought that they were totally indispensable
- couldn't be bothered working but turned up anyway
- thought they were the centre of the universe, and that the world revolved around them
- turned up late with all the excuses of the day
- could talk for Scotland but didn't do any work
- worked but did not communicate
- were miserable and wanted everyone else to be miserable
- thought they were part of one long tea break
- could look busy doing nothing
- were control freaks
- played one person off against another

A Mindful Culture

When organisations or departments within a company are managed well and support a healthy culture of positivity and wellbeing, you can see a noted difference on how people act, work performance and the overall atmosphere.

I was fortunate enough to work with a great leader who always made things clear about which direction we were going in and we all travelled together on this clear and prominent road, which was well defined. He set the parameters and everyone in the department knew where the boundaries lay, as we all had set criteria for all eventualities. When he left, however, and the department was taken over by someone new, everything seemed to be in disarray. It was like travelling along a road covered in black ice which had not been gritted, slipping from one car crash to the next with no brakes and no direction. When you are working in an environment which is poorly led, chaotic and branded as incompetent, you tend to be tarred with the same brush.

Sensory Overload

Sometimes life becomes just too much to handle. It's a bit like sensory overload and there is just too much to process. It can resemble the advertisements on television. The sound becomes louder, and we are bombarded with messages which demand us to buy these products – now! For example, food adverts for hamburgers, curries, pizzas. It can be too much to digest when you have just finished eating your evening meal. It's almost like running a marathon and immediately being told to run the 100 metres race without the chance to rest and recuperate. Personal relationships can be the same. They can be totally overwhelming, draining and difficult to manage.

Good Company

On the other hand, however, there is nothing more refreshing than spending time with someone who enjoys your company, lifts your spirits and treats you with mutual respect. Positive relationships are key to happiness and resilience, enhancing our lives. It really nurtures your soul when you find people that you can totally relate to and just be yourself. It means so much to have these wonderful people in your life who respect your individuality, personality and values. There is no hidden agenda, and you can discuss everything and anything with them without being judged. They hold your confidence as you hold theirs and although there are no set criteria, you both know and respect the boundaries. The gap is just right, and you feel totally at ease in their company. These acquaintances are the personification of mindfulness itself. It pays to nurture good friendships in your life. Mindfulness has provided me with the opportunity to view my life from a different vantage point and appreciate the people who have given me the opportunity to grow spiritually, intellectually and emotionally.

Mindfulness has taught me to cherish those wonderful, inspirational characters who encouraged me to flourish. Their energy, wisdom and sincerity will always be with me.

Don't dwell on those who
let you down. Cherish
those who lift you up!

Mindfulness Practice – Compassionate Image

Compassionate Image mindfulness meditation practice – **Appendix C**

Also available as a podcast at https://youtube.com/@eleanor-mindfulness

*Names have been changed to protect the identity of individuals.

Chapter 4

Rebuilding Yourself

I speak from the heart when I say that mindfulness has quite literally saved my life.

Mindfulness opens a whole new chapter. It helps us to discover how our minds work.

> *'...meditation is like having all the king's horses and all the king's men trying to put Humpty Dumpty together again'* (Chopra, 2020, p.14).

Upsetting Experiences

If you find yourself continuously going over the same story and bringing the upsetting scene to the foreground of your mind, you are, in fact, reliving the destructive memory over and over. It's like the news bulletins on television that go around in a cycle and feed you the same drastic stories.

> *'We know that memories, if vivid enough, bring back the emotions of the original circumstances that created the memory, often with an intense recollection of pain'* (Chopra, 2020, p.62).

When I was promoting my book *Mindfulness the Journey, Not the Destination* at Merchant Square in Glasgow, a gentleman approached me and said that he had served as a soldier in Northern Ireland and that he suffered from post-traumatic stress disorder, due to the scenes that he had personally witnessed. He said that he could cope most days when he was surrounded by kind and understanding people, like his family. However, the time he struggled the most was in the middle of the night when he was alone, and his mind was in turmoil.

I could totally relate to his anguish, as it is when I am alone or in company that I feel uncomfortable in, that I struggle. I think we all need a strong support network to help us to stay on track along with our mindfulness training.

> *'The power of your mind is unlimited and you can use it to your advantage by restoring and reinforcing optimal wellness – or to your disadvantage by undermining your health on every level'* (Brown, 2010, p.177).

Lightening the Load

I have discovered that when I carry out tasks that I do not enjoy, my mood state changes dramatically. I now make a conscious effort to make each task more enjoyable by using my senses, e.g. listening to uplifting music, using my favourite scent by lighting a perfumed candle, being able to glance at the sky or introducing my favourite colour into my day.

Remember to make a conscious effort to make any unpleasant tasks more enjoyable by introducing something that lightens your mood whilst you are carrying out this chore. It also helps to tune in with your posture, as when the body slumps, the mind slumps also.

Objectivity

Mindfulness provides the opportunity to see your life from a new platform. Instead of becoming your thoughts and emotions, you can regard them from a viewing platform. Almost like a performer, viewing the audience from an elevated stage.

'So training in mindfulness and acceptance enables us to step back and gain some degree of objectivity in relation to what is going on. And then, once we are in this witnessing mode, we are able to relate to what we are experiencing with kindness and compassion' (Gilbert and Choden, 2013, p.232).

The Relationship with Ourselves

The most important relationship we have in life is with ourselves and that is where mindfulness really comes into its own, enabling us to recognise our thoughts, feelings and emotions. We all need purpose and meaning in our lives and to recognise what is important to us. It is really worthwhile to write things down and work on our health and wellbeing and resilience. Our psychological, physiological, societal and financial wellbeing all contribute to our quality of life and how we view the world in which we live.

'Making time to invest into your well-being will boost your overall health and resilience and you will be better equipped to face life's challenges' (Webb, 2013, p.xvii).

Psychological Wellbeing

What we focus on we give energy to; therefore, our psychological wellbeing can improve our way of thinking, our thinking process and how we respond to others. Taking time to invest in our psychological wellbeing can affect, not only us, but also the people we share our lives with. Perhaps we are spending time on things in our lives which zap our energy and leave us feeling depleted. For example, we may be spending every evening watching soap operas with dark and depressing storylines. We may find that after an hour of being subjected to the trials and tribulations of the main characters, we have no energy to deal with challenges in our own life's drama.

Physiological Wellbeing

Our physiological wellbeing involves keeping fit and active in our daily lives. If we spend each day sitting on a train, sitting at a desk and then sitting in front of the TV, we may not even realise that we haven't taken any opportunity to exercise and keep our body active. This can lead to many health issues. Taking time to keep ourselves moving, as best we can, will lead to us feeling healthier and happier.

Just taking time to be in the great outdoors and taking a leisurely walk in the clear air can actually help your way of thinking. We don't have to torture ourselves with rigorous workouts that exhaust and deplete us. Spending time to find out what works for you, your schedule and your environment can really benefit your life.

Societal Wellbeing

Our societal wellbeing pertains to friendships, hobbies, interests and people we care for and organisations we are involved with. Perhaps it's time to take a fresh look at our friendships and invest more time with people who lift our spirits. Taking the opportunity to take up some new hobbies that will keep the mind and body as active as possible can have huge benefits to our overall health and wellbeing.

Showing an interest in the area in which you live can be so rewarding. There could be some places or buildings in your town, that others travel a great distance to see, that you haven't even visited. Gaining local knowledge of what historical background exists in your area can help you feel more connected. Investing time with people you care for can be so uplifting. Sharing a common interest can help to strengthen bonds with those you are closest to.

Financial Wellbeing

Our overall wellbeing can also be deeply affected by our financial wellbeing. Keeping a close eye on our household budgeting can help us prioritise where our hard-earned cash is allocated. It really is rewarding to spend some time looking at ways that you can save some money just by a few lifestyle tweaks.

In the fictional book, *Confessions of a Shopaholic* (Kinsella, 2003), the main character spends more than she earns before she reaches the office. By the time she has paid for the cappuccino, carry-out breakfast, magazine to read on the commute and window shopping, she has built up a huge amount of debt. Although the main character in this publication is fictitious, I have personally watched people live and spend like this and then wonder why their financial status is in jeopardy. Perhaps getting up 15 minutes earlier we could save a few pounds by breakfasting at home and taking the opportunity to practise mindfulness on the train or bus en route to work.

I would also be aware of buying things to make you happy or lift your mood. Previously, I was very guilty of doing this just to cheer myself up. I thought that I could make myself happier by buying that new dress, coat or handbag. Mindfulness teaches us that we cannot buy happiness.

Energy

> *'...depression and low mood undermine us by robbing us of the energy to do the things that would nourish us the most'* (Williams, Teasdale, Segal, and Kabat-Zinn, 2007, p.203/204).

Prolonged stress, trauma and emotional stress can weaken the body's energy centres making it weaker and more susceptible to illness. Maintaining balance in the body's energy system is vital for physical, emotional and spiritual wellbeing. Physical illness and pain are often due to imbalances within the body's energy systems.

It is important to look after our physical energy by making sure that we eat a balanced diet, exercise regularly and get enough sleep.

Emotional Energy

> *'Gratitude is an immense source of emotional energy'* (Draper, 2012, p.87).

Mindfulness aids us in being grateful for what we have in this moment. Instead of hankering after what we don't have, we are more appreciative of what we do have. When we focus on the negative it drains our energy and can make us feel depleted. Try starting each day with an attitude of gratitude. Keeping a gratitude diary can also help us to realise what we have to be thankful for, in this moment.

Mental Energy

We can regulate our mental energy through our mindfulness practise. Allow the stillness and meditation of your practise to energise your mental status. Instead of the mind being constantly busy, we can take the time out to just simply rest in awareness. When we do our mindfulness practise regularly, we begin to realise that we are not losing time by meditating but, in many instances, we are gaining time because we discover that we have the clarity of thought which enables us to act more wisely.

Spiritual Energy

Mindfulness is spiritual and:

> *'Spiritual energy is what gathers everything else together'* (Draper, 2012, p.88). Spiritual does not necessarily need to involve any religious following but is more related to a person's soul or spirituality. The Dalai Lama advises that:

> *'...whether a person is a religious believer does not matter much. Far more important is that they be a good human being'* (cited by Armstrong, 2011, p.20).

Mindfulness can help to align and harmonise all our energy centres enabling us to live a more balanced and fulfilling life.

Mindfulness has helped me to focus on goodness and kindness, and I hope that I can make a positive contribution to the world in which I live by setting clear, structured goals for the future where mindfulness is at the heart of my raison d'être.

But it is worth noting that:

> *'Without a sense of purpose you will struggle to renew or to expend energy well'* (Draper, 2012, p.88).

Mindfulness Practice – A Safe Place

A Safe Place mindfulness meditation practice – **Appendix D**

Also available as a podcast at https://youtube.com/@eleanor-mindfulness

Chapter 5
A Sense of Purpose

In a Rut

We all need a sense of purpose in life. This is what gets us up in the morning and helps us to keep going forward with strength, enthusiasm and motivation. If you have been through painful or disruptive experiences in your life, it is all too easy to focus only on the stressful event and not see beyond it. Personally, I got stuck in this rut and struggled even to get out of bed in the morning. Sometimes it can feel as if you are a little rabbit caught in car headlights, and you totally freeze and struggle to move forward. Through experience, I think it is best to take small steps to get your life back on track. You may be holding on to grudges and disappointments from the past which are restricting you from progressing in your life.

> '*...our minds like to hold on to wounds, and fashion a sense of identity from them*' (Draper, 2012, p.65).

Transition

I was very fortunate to spend many years of my life in a profession that I loved and flourished in. The job I had was so worthwhile, rewarding and made a huge impact to people's lives. Saving lives on our roads by taking a pro-active approach to road safety was the clear aim and objective of my work and enthusing others to do the same through encouragement, education, enforcement and engineering. I felt part of a community with the same definitive aims, objectives and direction, which gave me a strong sense of purpose. However, the powers that be decided that my job was no longer necessary, and my job, team and budget were taken from me. I found it very difficult to get my life back on track. My mindfulness practise gave me the clarity and energy to reassess my life and find my new sense of purpose. Life is challenging and even more so when you're not in the driving seat. My life's journey at this point took me to the beautiful Samye Ling Tibetan Buddhist Temple at Eskdalemuir in the picturesque Scottish Borders to study mindfulness. Spending time to just 'simply be' can have a spiritual and profound impact on your life.

> *'The main point in meditating is to achieve some clarity. Then we will automatically do what is right in our lives'* (Chöje Lama Yeshe Losal Rinpoche, 2014, p.56).

Samye Ling's tranquillity energised me and provided me with the strength and purpose I was looking for to move forward from the feeling of loss and bewilderment when my career came to a sudden halt. Spending time with wonderful likeminded people can uplift you. It is a bit like pressing the refresh button on your computer. Visiting the peaceful and majestic Holy Isle off Arran in the west of Scotland brought back my sense of purpose and made me feel alive again. The mindfulness practises with the MSc students studying at the University of Aberdeen brought enrichment to my days. Attending the wonderful, historical building of the University of Aberdeen also had an immense impact on me. Learning that the university was established in 1495 and knowing that students had been studying there from the 15th century really inspired me.

I continued on this amazing mindfulness journey and completed my MSc in Studies in Mindfulness in 2018. I decided to focus my dissertation on a subject that I felt passionate about, road safety; *The Potential Influence of Sustained Mindfulness Practise on*

Driver Behaviour. My research clearly showed that sustained mindfulness practise can have a positive effect on driver attitude and behaviour. The generated evidence gathered in my study proved that mindfulness impacts positively on attention, awareness, observation, compassion and emotional regulation. My dissertation provided an insight into mindfulness as a potential behavioural change technique, within a driving context, which could lead to enhanced safety on our roads.

Listening to others on this mindfulness journey and realising that mindfulness can change so many lives for the better helped me to move forward with passion and enthusiasm. It was an enormous feat for me to take and complete the MSc journey at this stage in my life due to lack of confidence in my ability. It was a very steep learning curve, and I have gained so much from completing this course of study. In my first year, I put a great deal of effort into my reports but struggled with critical analysis and interpreting research papers. This was a completely new way of study for me. Sometimes, however, embarking on a new project can reignite the spark within you and help you to overcome all fears.

Facing your Fears

One of the most challenging things along my journey was to address my three greatest fears. I have always been terrified of wasps, fire and heights. These fears were due to past conditioning and stemmed from my childhood years. Through my mindfulness journey, I was able to face all of these fears. My first visit to Samye Ling in September 2015 entailed outdoor meditation practises. We had to sit in silence outside the eco cabin and practise our mindfulness of breathing. As we sat there, wasps began circling around our heads. As I had never met any of the group of people before, I knew that I had to comply with the stillness and silence, which I found very difficult when surrounded by the menacing and distracting buzzing of insects. However, as I focused on my breathing, I was able to overcome my fear. Also at Samye Ling, we were asked to light tealights in the butterlamp house which

I managed to do along with my lovely classmates. I discovered that although my heart was racing, tummy churning and hands were shaking, if I focused on my breathing I could carry out the task in hand. It's amazing how you can face your fears when you are surrounded by kind and compassionate people. On my visit to the Holy Isle, we climbed to the top of the highest point on the island, Mulloch Mòr, where the views of Ailsa Craig and the beautiful Ayrshire coastline stretch out magnificently before you. My fear of heights kicked in halfway up the hill and my legs began to tremble but with the help, assistance and encouragement of my peers, I managed to climb all the way to the top. Having people to help you in life is so refreshing and these people, in my opinion, are mindfulness personified.

Many of our fears are due to conditioning brought on by experiences starting from early childhood and, with the right encouragement and support, it is possible to overcome our worst fears. Mindfulness helps us to address our fears by letting us realise where they stem from and understanding the significance and true reality of the situation.

Your Purpose in Life

Knowing the things that you are naturally good at doing can be a good guide to finding your true purpose. My advice is to start small and gradually work towards what truly brings you the strength and zest for life.

Your sense of purpose maybe to learn new skills that are meaningful to you or to be more creative and take forward a new project. Finding something that you genuinely like and care deeply about will ignite the spark which will take you in the right direction so that you feel that you are making a positive contribution to your world. Who knows where your journey will lead? It's a journey of self-discovery where you will truly find a sense of fulfilment by realising what you feel passionately about.

Getting to Know You

Write down three things that you value most in life.	
Write down three interests that you have.	
Write down three things that you are talented in.	
Write down three things that make you feel happy.	
Write down three things that you care about in life.	
What are your main strengths?	
What skills do you have?	
What do you desire most in life?	

Now look closely at all your answers and see if there is a theme which exists which will lead you to finding your true sense of purpose.

One of my friends completed this table and found the main themes were happiness, travel and dancing. My friend is now following a dream of being a dance host on a cruise ship and dancing around the world – a true sense of purpose.

Chapter 6
Gratitude

The Grass is Green

We've probably all heard the saying *'the grass is always greener on the other side'* but our mindfulness practise teaches us that this is not always the case. This saying is believed to be based on the quote,

> *'The harvest is always richer in another man's field'* (Ovid, 1BC).

When we practise mindfulness, we begin to realise that our field is, in fact, green, healthy and lush. We become aware of all the good things present in our life that we can be grateful for, instead of focusing on what we don't have.

We are Here

Once we embark on this mindfulness journey, we realise that we have indeed already arrived.

> *'We are all looking, if we are honest, for a path home to the very heart of life itself'* (Draper, 2012, p.20).

Mindfulness lets us see that we are already home in this moment. Through mindfulness practise we can find our true, authentic, self.

> *'Some people dig around to find out who they are, like they're looking for the toy in the Christmas cracker of their psyche'* (Wax, 2018, p.30).

When we introduce mindfulness into our daily lives, the searching can stop as we realise that we have already found ourselves in this precious moment.

The Ego

We find that if we can let go of the egotistical person we have become, we can then shine a torch into our very soul. We tend to define ourselves by our status in society. This status seems to be embedded in ego and not on our soul. Our ego is a facet we build up to face the world, almost like a defence mechanism. Mindfulness helps us to see ourselves as we really are.

The Power to See our True Self

> *'O wad some Pow'r the giftie gie us.*
> *To see oursels as ithers see us!'*
>
> (Burns, 1786)

I believe that mindfulness is that very power. Mindfulness enables us to see ourselves more clearly and understand our true identity – warts and all! This allows us to work on our being with kindness and compassion and to unfold our basic goodness. We may have been conditioned to always look on the dark side of life and not realise that there is a bright side. I have found that mindfulness is an ongoing process of reconditioning myself to face life's situations with a greater sense of reality.

The Soul

I feel that mindfulness is like shining a torch into my very soul to uncover my true nature. The soul will not compromise.

> *'It does not seek its identity in material possessions as the ego does, nor does it require us to finish first and get all the glory in life'* (Draper, 2012, p.26).

Mindfulness teaches us to simply be in the present moment.

> *'The present is a soulful place'* (Draper, 2012, p.57).

Positivity

Looking towards gratitude with a sense of positivity can help us to appreciate the goodness in our life. When we act positively and bring positive actions into our lives it can increase our sense of gratitude. One of the most moving experiences in my life involved helping people who had almost given up all hope in moving forward. Encouraging others to appreciate the basic things in life and adopt a positive approach to the simple and pleasurable aspects that exist in the present moment, increases our sense of gratitude. I was deeply moved by their appreciation and this, in turn, gave me such a sense of gratitude in what I already have, here and now, in this moment.

Positivity comes with an outlook of 'glass half full' instead of 'glass half empty' attitude. Spending time with kind and compassionate people, with a positive outlook, can lift your spirits and enthuse you to keep going with an attitude of gratitude.

Negativity

We are all guilty of holding on to negative things and experiences from the past. We may be harbouring grudges, resentment, deceitfulness, sorrow or bitterness that really, in this present moment, is not serving us any purpose.

> *'We attach ourselves mentally to all kinds of things and hoard them in our mental lofts'* (Draper, 2012 p.65).

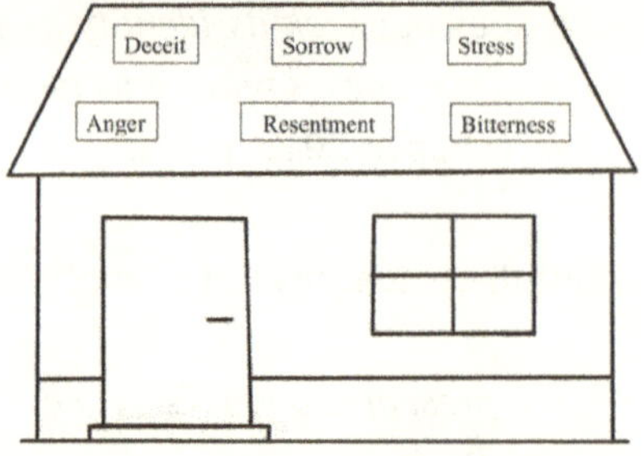

It is a good idea to look at what negative baggage we are hoarding and, through our meditation practise, learn to release these. This will enable us to flourish just like the lotus flower which blossoms from all the mud and cloudiness below the surface of the pond. This is not about denial or rejection but by practising mindfulness we can learn to release the hold that past experiences can have on us.

The Lotus Flower

Our mindfulness practise will let us realise that no matter what bad experiences we have encountered on our life's journey, we can still manage to flourish.

The beautiful lotus flower above the surface is the part of us that flourishes and has all our positive experiences. Isn't it truly amazing that this wonderful lotus flower can reveal itself in all its glory from the murkiest of ponds.

Creating your own Lotus Flower

Appreciating all the positive things that exist in our lives can help us to embark on a journey to complete the aspirations we have been longing to fulfil.

On a blank piece of paper draw a lotus flower similar to the image opposite. Then write on each petal all the positive things that exist in your life. Continue to add to the petals all the good things that you experience with a sense of gratitude.

Chapter 7
Being Yourself

Being True to Yourself

No matter what occupation we are in or how we choose to live our lives, it is vital that we are true to ourselves. Whether we are a world leader, financial adviser, gardener, chef, pilot or baker, mindfulness helps us to develop our own identity with kindness and compassion.

Conscience

Our conscience pertains to our moral sense of what is right and what is wrong and guides us to behave in a certain way. I remember meeting a man on a cruise ship who was an identical twin. Both he and his twin brother were qualified civil engineers, but his brother always found it difficult to get a job due to his poor interview techniques. His twin brother attended an interview for him and got the job, and he was appointed as a civil engineer with the organisation. I often wonder how either of them can be true to themselves or whether their conscience bothers them about this at any time.

I have often read about people sitting driving tests on behalf of other people. I really worry about the impact this could have in terms of safety on our roads.

I knew a girl who used to enter competitions for plant growing, knitting, crochet and painting. She told me that she got her friends to do the work and then submitted the projects as her own work.

These may seem like extreme examples of people not being true towards themselves or others, but we are presently hearing of circumstances of people using artificial intelligence to fraudulently gain qualifications. It is very concerning to think of professions where a person's health is dependent on someone who may not have the knowledge or skills to treat them due to their falsified academic certifications.

Finding Yourself

> *'...the spirit of meditation, which emphasizes being your own person and understanding what it means to be yourself'* (Kabat-Zinn, 2013, p.25).

You may find that somewhere along your life's journey that you have lost yourself. It could feel like someone has been chiselling away at a lump of marble and created the person that you have now become, based on their own design. It's a bit like a stonemason carving out a figure which you would not choose for yourself. If this is the case, how do you find yourself again?

The way I have managed to resculpt myself using my mindfulness practise is to realise that:

> *'You need the past that you have; it is raw clay on the potter's wheel'* (Kabat-Zinn, 2017, p.16).

With an open mind and heart, we can learn so much from the past. My past has taught me many things about life, and I know that I can begin to resculpt myself so that I can be a positive force in the world.

> *'...in order to become virtuoso human beings, we have to begin by understanding our basic nature – the clay, so to speak, with which we're given to work'* (Tsoknyi Rinpoche and Swanson, 2012, p.39).

Past Conditioning

You may have been told by others that you are not good at certain things and have convinced yourself that this is the case. I remember being told by a guidance teacher, at a school that I was working at, that applying for a job three grades above the one I was doing was really about *'having thoughts above my station'* and that perhaps I needed to aim a little lower. Past conditioning can blur our vision and curtail our progress. Mindfulness teaches us what is really true about who we are and what we can do. You may have been told that you are a replica of another family member. You will have heard phrases such as *'oh, he's just like his dad'*. Whether you look like another family member or not, does not take away the fact that you are unique and that nurture can prove to be stronger than nature when it comes to family traits.

Uniqueness

I used to watch a programme on TV where people would appear and tell the presenter who they were going to be, e.g. Elvis, Kylie Minogue, Neil Diamond, Michael Bublé, Lulu or Madonna. Their performances were so convincing that they looked, sounded and performed just like the real stars. I knew of someone who performed tribute nights as Elvis but even when I saw him during the day he was still dressed as Elvis, looked like Elvis and talked like Elvis. I think he believed that he was, in fact, Elvis.

I also know people that can change drastically into another character depending on what company they are in. I worked with a formidable lady who used to come out with the saying *'he has got more faces than the town clock'*.

I think, in the past, I was guilty of this myself, especially with people in authority. I would become mouse-like, nervous and shy and unable to speak.

Our mindfulness practise helps us to realise our unique self. We discover that we don't have to pretend to be someone else. We can just be ourselves. We don't need a script or to be someone else's understudy in the play of life.

> *'Choosing to invest in your highest self is like unlocking the door to your true potential. Why settle for imitation when you can be an original masterpiece?'* (Azur, 2024).

The Interior Decorator

> *'You are the interior decorator of your life'* (Wax, 2018, p.104).

I love this quote by Ruby Wax, and I am sure it will inspire so many people. I have used this quote so many times to motivate myself and others along this mindfulness journey, as it helps us to recognise the fact that we have so many choices open to us on a daily basis. Through mindfulness, we are more aware and awake to these choices and this, in turn, opens up a whole new world for us.

I think it is great when we can put our own stamp on things and use our own interpretation of the quote to motivate us to live our lives in a better way. One of the participants in my mindfulness class took her view on the subject quite literally. She returned home and cleared out a spare room which had been unusable for years due to the mountain of clutter and discarded items which the family had accumulated. She cleared out all the items and took them to the charity shop, gave the room a lick of paint, designed a meditation cushion and curtains and used the room for study and meditation purposes. The entire family were amazed by her sudden and purposeful actions and were deeply moved by her positive change in direction at a very challenging time in her life.

By Yourself

I know now that I do have to take time out of my busy schedule to just be me and feel grounded. In the past, I always felt that I had to be with other people constantly. I never took time to spend alone.

Finding peace in your own solitude, from time to time, can help to refresh and restore you.

Being yourself and not the replica of someone else is key to a life well lived. Taking time to just be by yourself can help to nourish, calm and recharge the mind, body and spirit and replenish your energy levels helping you to be the wonderful, genuine and unique person that you have become through your mindfulness practise.

Chapter 8
Life Changes

Impermanence

Impermanence is something that we are made so aware of through our mindfulness practise. Our lives are constantly changing, and we are faced with so many different challenges every day. Every change in our life has a knock-on effect on the people we encounter along life's journey.

The Times of our Lives

The birth of a child can be such a wonderful experience in our lives but adapting to this new life brings extreme challenges: coping with sleepless nights, extra responsibility and added expense can put a great deal of pressure on any relationship. It can affect extended relationships within the family with relatives giving their expert advice on how to nurture the child. Conflicting views on feeding, bathing, comforting, dressing and raising your child can be totally confusing and add to the initial stress.

Starting school can be quite a tearful experience for both parent and child. It may be that the child has not spent a great deal of time in other children's company and therefore being confronted by all these other children with their different personalities, needs and priorities can be a bit overwhelming.

Adolescence is another life change which can bring about problems. Hormonal changes and finding where you fit in can be quite daunting. Maintaining healthy relationships at this stage in our lives can seem like the hardest task that we have ever encountered.

Getting engaged to be married can be an exciting and positive time in our lives, when we realise that we enjoy our partner's company and being together seems to be our main priority. Making plans and enthusing about the future with positivity and mutual enthusiasm may lead us to see our life through rose-tinted glasses.

Marriage is one of life's big events which doesn't come without its problems. The wedding itself can, in some cases, be like a fairytale but once, as a couple, you're faced with the responsibilities of running and maintaining and funding a home together, it can really take its toll. So many marriages end in divorce, and this can be such a harrowing and costly business which can have a devastating effect and serious long-lasting impacts on so many lives.

Moving house is another one of the most stressful things that we can encounter in our lives. The planning, disruption and expense can lead to stress and a great deal of anxiety. Once you move, you may find that all in the garden is not rosy as more work is required than first anticipated. Becoming accustomed to your new environment can take a bit of adjustment.

When we are faced with health issues in our lives it can be quite easy for us to blame ourselves for our ailments, but many illnesses are not of our own making and can be hereditary or caused by the environment.

Losing our job can reach a high point on the stress scale and can leave us feeling inadequate. Writing down and focusing on all of our positive attributes can help us to build our confidence and reassure us that there is a positive way forward in our working life.

Losing a loved one brings its own heartache, stress and an immense feeling of loss. It is an occasion that we all need to take time to grieve and come to terms with. It feels like a huge void has appeared in our lives. At times we feel that our heart is totally broken and will never mend.

When we look at any one of these life-changing events it can be daunting but when several of them happen in quick succession, it can be totally overwhelming.

Finding calm in a frantic world may seem like an impossible feat, but mindfulness can help us to find that inner calm and inner peace which will help us to cope in every situation in our lives no matter what stage we are at or where we are.

Resilience

By practising mindfulness on a regular basis, we are building up reserves of energy for when we need it most. It's a bit like charging up your own internal battery with energy and resilience which can then be available for use when most needed. Therefore, when life throws us its challenges, we are more able to cope.

By enhancing our personal resilience, we can look at our thoughts, feelings and beliefs and find our true identity. We learn what our attitudes to certain things in life are and how we perceive things with meaning, purpose and a sense of worth. By optimising our living environment to best serve our needs we can enrich the way in which we live.

We all need a sense of belonging in our own lives and mindfulness helps us to recognise where we belong in this beautiful world of ours by encouraging us to look at nature and the miracle of growth and development of each season. By engaging with nature within our mindfulness practise we truly have a sense of being alive and connected to our surroundings.

> *'We each have the option to choose to align ourselves with the highest principles, to strive to fulfil the highest possible vision of ourselves and to endeavour to be kind, loving and compassionate to all forms of life, including our own'* (Brown, 2010, p.225).

Time

The most precious gift we have been given is time. Time means more to us than any material things. Time well spent is so worthwhile. Time is the most precious gift that you can give to others who appreciate your company. How do we spend our time?

The time we spend practising mindfulness is time well spent as this is a time that we can call our own. It really does personify what we really mean by the phrase 'me time'.

Now is the Time

Time to talk and time to care,
Time to know you're always there.
Time to heal and time to smile,
Time to walk that extra mile.

Time to wish you'd never leave,
Time to hold and time to grieve.
Time that travels very fast,
Time that takes too long to pass.

Time to sing and time to dance,
Time to love, a fine romance.
Daytime, nighttime, good times, bad times
Before you know, it turns to past times.

Time to remember, time to forget,
Time to move on and time to regret.
What time is it? I hear you say.
The time is 'now' but slips away.

by Eleanor Gibson

Precious Time

Now that we realise how precious time is, it makes sense to look at the ways we spend our time.

Fill in the pie chart below, based on how you spend your hours on an average day.

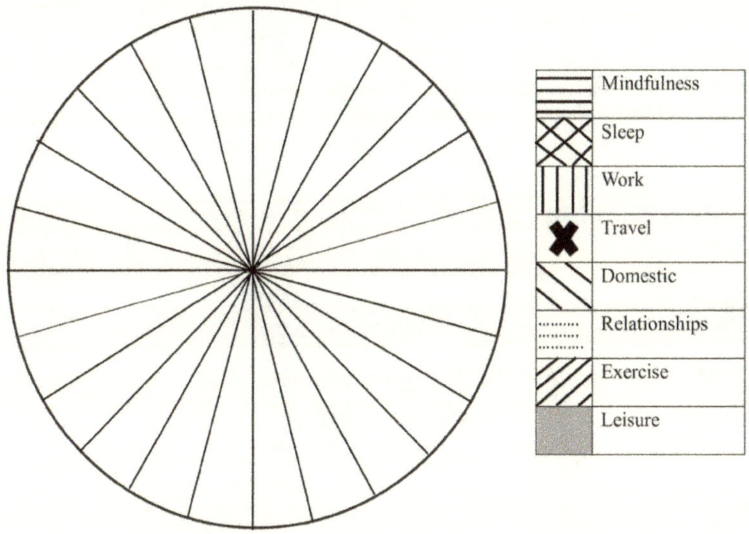

Now examine the pie chart and see if you can prioritise your use of your precious time into a healthier and more worthwhile balance.

Now complete the pie chart below with a healthier balance.

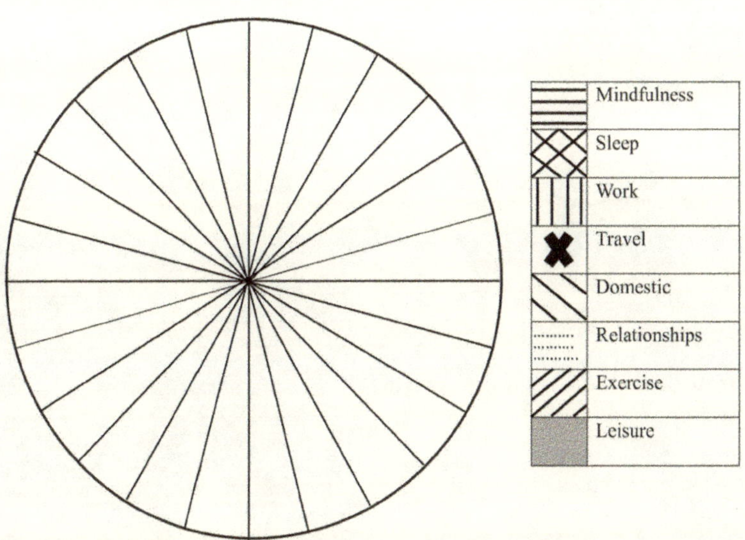

Chapter 9

The Benefits of Mindfulness

I would like to share with you some of the benefits of mindfulness, using quotes from the authors who have inspired me along my mindfulness journey. Their words reassure and motivate me to continue travelling on this amazing mindful journey of life. Their experience and insights have been so beneficial in reinforcing what I have discovered for myself from my mindfulness practise.

Perception

> *'...mindfulness actually changes the brain and our perceptions of the world around us'* (Yates, 2017, p.xi).

Before I took up practising mindfulness, I used to rush around like a headless chicken, not realising the beautiful and amazing world around me. I did not take the time to appreciate the miracle of growth and change to be found in nature. Even when I went for a walk it was always about the destination and finishing point. I did not take time to be in the moment and really look at this wonderful place we live in, called earth.

Isn't it amazing how the sun rises every morning and sets each night. The wonderful transformation of the moon as it waxes and wanes, how awesome! We have so much to learn from nature. No matter what stage we are at in our lives, we can use nature as our guide. Through mindfulness, I realise that even in my most difficult days in life, if nature can refresh each day, then so can I.

Contentment

> *'Contentment means that we experience a sense of fulfilment and joy. If we're content, then we're rich even if we only have a few dollars in our wallet. But if we have no contentment, then we'll suffer even with a million dollars under our mattress'* (Dzogchen Ponlop, 2011, p.56).

Mindfulness helps us to realise that we don't really need a lot of material things to make us happy and contented. Before I introduced mindfulness into my daily life, I would buy things to cheer myself up but found that the feeling would fade very quickly and not have the long-lasting effect that I was hoping for. We learn to find that it is the small things in life that actually mean most to us. It pays to spend time on the simple things in life that lift your spirits. It can be the smallest thing like smelling your favourite soap, enjoying a cup of tea, listening to soothing music or wearing your favourite colour.

Wisdom

Andrew Olendzki states:

> *'We don't really have much influence on how we see or hear things, how we perceive them, or how they feel to us. All these are dealt each moment off the top of the deck, so to speak; our main job is to learn how to play the hand skillfully'* (cited in Germer and Siegel, 2012, p.123).

In other words,

> *'There will always be some aspect of the full catastrophe to be faced somewhere, sometime. It is* how *you face it that matters'* (Kabat-Zinn, 2013, p.507).

Life is challenging and we, as human beings, can be our own worst enemies by making situations more difficult and troublesome for ourselves. If we practise mindfulness, on a daily basis, we start to realise that we can have that calmness and clarity of thought which will make life easier by helping us to make wiser decisions which will benefit us, not just in this moment, but for our future as well. Before I took up mindfulness, I seemed to be in a constant state of confusion, and this led to me making decisions and carrying out actions which I later regretted.

Self-love

> *'Because mindfulness is one of the core components of self-compassion, when we improve our mindfulness skills, we automatically increase our ability to be self-compassionate'* (Neff, 2015, p.101).

I think the most important lesson we learn from mindfulness in our lives is that love and compassion start with ourselves. Taking time each day to show kindness towards ourselves, in my opinion, is a key factor in living a healthy life. Being our own best friend is important. Carrying out kind tasks towards yourself, the way you would towards a best friend, lets you begin to value the wonderful and unique person that you are. When you start to uncover the goodness and warmth within your soul you then can extend this goodness and warmth towards others.

I used to be such a people-pleaser and always put everyone else first in every situation. This led to exhaustion, frustration and resentment. You begin to realise that not everyone appreciates you going that extra mile for them and this can lead to feelings of failure and disappointment. The big realisation is that you should love yourself first and cultivate the amazing person that you are.

> *'When we give ourselves compassion, the tight knot of negative self-judgement starts to dissolve, replaced by a feeling of peaceful, connected acceptance – a sparkling diamond that emerges from the coal'* (Neff, 2015, p.13).

Clarity

> *'You're fully present, happier, and at ease, because you're not so easily caught up in the stories and melodramas the mind likes to concoct'* (Yates, Immergut and Graves, 2017, p.38).

Before finding mindfulness, I used to work myself into a state of confusion, even when my life was running along smoothly. I would constantly confuse matters with 'what ifs' and 'worse case scenarios', to the point where I couldn't think straight and worked myself into a frenzy. Mindfulness helps you to see things as they really are, giving you clarity of vision.

> *'Mindfulness is often likened to a mirror; it simply reflects what is there'* (Rosenberg and Guy, 1998, p.15).

I am now able to work on the true facts as they unfold, instead of the soap opera that I thought and believed to be the truth. The key lesson in this is to always be true to yourself.

Embodiment

Ash Ranpura says:

> *'Emotions aren't in a particular place, they come out of the communication between your brain and body. And that's a two-way street, so if you're depressed, even your muscles work differently from when you're in a good mood. For example, posture really affects emotions'* (cited in Wax, 2018, p.59).

This is a very important lesson we learn in mindfulness. I used to get really anxious and discovered that my shoulders tensed up, my breathing became shallow and even my feet ached. When you embark on your mindfulness journey, you realise that by changing your posture you can change the way you think and the way you think changes your posture. I used to slump over my desk and before

I knew it my mind would start to slump also. By checking in with our posture throughout the day we can change our mindset and give ourselves energy and positivity in order to function more effectively and efficiently. Mindfulness also teaches us that the breath is a great healer. When we feel sluggish and tired, we can energise ourselves by focusing more on the inbreath. Taking a few deep breaths will bring more oxygen into the body providing us with the much-needed energy we require. On the other hand, if we are feeling tense and stressed, we can calm the mind and body by focusing more on our outbreath. The mind and body are always working together.

> *'There is compelling evidence that the state of your mind affects the state of your body and, more specifically, that emotions influence physiology and therefore health'* (Davidson and Begley, 2013, p.132).

Peace

> *'If you truly want to discover a lasting sense of peace and contentment, you need to learn to rest your mind'* (Yongey Mingyur Rinpoche and Swanson, 2009, p.125).

Practising mindfulness on a regular basis provides that inner peace in a frantic world which some days seems to be spiralling out of control. It provides the solace which we all so desperately need to help us cope with all of life's challenges. The sense of serenity gained whilst sitting on a cushion practising mindfulness will be with us long after we have completed our meditation practise.

Gratitude

> *'Research suggests that practising gratitude is one of the most reliable ways of increasing happiness'* (Sinclair and Seydel, 2013, p.185).

Every morning, when I wake up, I think of three things that I am grateful for. I write these things in a journal. It is the first three things that come to mind. For example, eyesight, hearing, mobility, food, clothes, friends and the weather. It's an amazing feeling when you focus on gratitude and really appreciate what you have in this moment.

Balance

> *'Finding our internal speed limit involves a process of first recognizing our thoughts, feelings, and physical sensations as part of the ongoing process of being alive and then learning to discover a balance among them'* (Tsoknyi Rinpoche and Swanson, 2012, p.160).

One of the first things you learn when you start to practise mindfulness is the wandering mind. Through practise, we then recognise where our mind wanders to. We also become more aware of our feelings and where we are holding onto those feelings within the body. Mindfulness teaches us to adopt a healthier relationship with our thoughts, feelings and emotions and where we experience these in the body. We are then in a position to achieve a sense of balance and equilibrium. In other words, we don't have to become our thoughts, feelings and emotions but make friends with them and take a levelled approach.

> *'You have to find a balance between tension and relaxation'* (Yongey Mingyur Rinpoche and Swanson, 2009, p.129).

In the past I was guilty of working all the hours I possibly could and some days I could almost meet myself coming back. I didn't take the time to relax and just simply be. I now know that the balance between work and leisure time is paramount.

Calmness

> *'When we are calm we take things in our stride. When we are calm the seesaw of highs and lows is level, and if it ever begins to tip one way or another it returns easily to the point of*

> *balance. To maintain that balance may require constant small adjustments one way or another, so being balanced or calm is an active state that we have to participate in and perhaps deliberately move toward'* (Black, 2018, p.174).

Mindfulness has brought the calmness that I so longed for into my world. I think it makes sense to instil a sense of calm into every situation. When we are calm, we are more likely to make wiser decisions which will inevitably affect our future. When the seesaw is tipped to the extreme it is far more difficult to return to the point of balance which benefits us the most.

Respect

> *'Just as mindfulness helps you learn to treat yourself with more kindness and respect, you begin to treat our human and animal families and the environment in which we live with the same kindness and respect'* (Sears, 2014, p.45).

I think building on your own self-respect is important, as how can you expect others to respect you, if you do not respect yourself. Mindfulness helps us to respect the person we are by getting to know ourselves and valuing and building on our positive attributes.

> *'Therefore, because you respect yourself, you do not have to depend on gain and victory. And because you trust yourself, it is unnecessary to be fearful of others'* (Chögyam Trungpa Rinpoche, 2015, p.124).

This respect gives us the confidence we require as we get to know ourselves and begin to trust our own judgements.

Focused

> *'Anchoring your attention in the breath does more than cultivate a focused, calm mind – it allows you to see how the mind works'* (Germer, 2009, p.49).

When our mind is in turmoil, we are unable to think straight or stay focused. When we focus on our breathing and use it as our anchor to ground us in the present moment we then see where our mind wanders to. When we do the body scan, we are training the mind to concentrate on what we choose to focus on and when the mind wanders, we can gently bring it back to the part of the body we are holding in full awareness. This enables us to be able to focus more easily and readily with our daily tasks and to recognise when we become distracted.

When you embark on this mindfulness journey you will begin to perceive life in a different light. The clarity, peace, compassion, self-love and gratitude you acquire will enrich your life in ways that you never thought possible. You will be able to focus on what is really important to you and this will enable you to find the respect, contentment and wisdom which will lead to a healthier and more balanced lifestyle.

Mindfulness for Everyone

The benefits of mindfulness can help us live healthier and compassionate lives no matter what age we are, or what challenges we are presently having to deal with.

If everyone could embrace mindfulness into their daily lives, this could impact on the entire world being mindful and compassionate, thereby enriching all our lives. If we could adopt Draper's view on 'less is more' (Draper, 2012), we could encourage each country to focus on what they have and not look to grasp more of what they haven't, this would help to enrich the lives of each country's inhabitants. By focusing on the good that exists in what we already have and sharing any overabundance with those that are genuinely struggling we could improve so many lives, for the better, throughout our world.

Chapter 10

Mindfulness – A Different Platform

It may seem at times in your life that no matter how much effort and goodness you put into it that there is always some form of the 'full catastrophe' to face (Kabat-Zinn, 2013). You could be floating on high like a butterfly one minute, but feel your life come crashing down the next and struggle to crawl forward. You may also feel, to a certain extent, that your experiences in life have dampened or damaged your enthusiasm and clouded your vision and that the bountiful vibrancy you once had has slipped away, leaving you feeling flat and demotivated.

Mindfulness – A Different Platform is a motivational book which helps us to realise how our mind works and that, through mindfulness practise, you will realise the importance of building on your own happiness and developing a more positive relationship with your moods, mind states and emotions. Training our mind to stay healthy, through mindfulness practise, will enable us to see the true reality of how we perceive things.

It is very difficult when you are faced with something in life that you find hard to process. Destructive relationships can harm our health and wellbeing and if you're not careful this can reach a point of no return. Mindfulness enables us to start right now, in this moment, to rebuild ourselves by recognising the importance of healthy relationships and 'minding the gap' as discussed in chapter three, in order to keep our individuality, moral standards and uniqueness. It is important to be aware of the company we keep and to allow ourselves to simply be ourselves. Learning to recognise what makes us happy is very important and sometimes we need to learn what makes us unhappy in order to know what really makes us feel good about our lives.

Mindfulness provides us with the clarity to see that we can all make choices to enrich our lives by finding our true, authentic self. Life is full of challenges, some good, some bad, but no matter what stage we are at in our life, we can all learn to view our life from a different vantage point through mindful awareness. The advantages we gain by introducing mindfulness into our daily lives are numerous and so rewarding.

It is all too easy to lose ourselves in others, but by learning to mind the gap in our relationships we will realise that perhaps the relationship with ourselves is one which is truly worth cultivating. Mindfulness will help us to improve our wellbeing and resilience and find that vital spark which will renew our energy and help us to get back on track and realise our true potential, enabling us to reignite our true passions and find our true sense of purpose.

We may at times believe that the grass is always greener on the other side but, by starting right now in this moment, with a positive outlook, we will realise through gratitude how much we have to be truly grateful for. By building on your uniqueness and realising what wonderful attributes you already have you will reach your higher self. Once we embark on this mindfulness journey, the benefits become apparent, and we can truly flourish just like the lotus flower. You can be, through your mindfulness practise, the interior decorator of your life (Wax, 2018).

> *'In a world where you can be anything, be yourself'* (Albert Einstein).

Mindfulness – A Different Platform provides that vantage point to get our lives back on track from this precious moment onwards.

'Nothing and no one is stopping us from living more lightly, more joyfully, more freely – apart from us, and the choices we make for ourselves' (Draper, 2012, P.130).

Afterword

I am writing this to tell you how my sister, Eleanor, who has written this book, helped me so much through a very difficult time in my life. Her understanding, patience and kindness mean so much to me. Both my husband and I were diagnosed with cancer within weeks of one another. I have suffered for years with chronic depression and anxiety so, as you can imagine, I took the whole situation very badly. We went through our cancer treatment together which entailed attending hospitals every week for months – consultations, blood tests and treatments. It was such a tough and harrowing time. My sister and her husband made sure that we didn't miss a single appointment. This enabled our son, Anthony, to attend his work which really was important for his livelihood, health and wellbeing. After all the treatment, I felt totally exhausted but also had difficulty doing all the things I used to do.

Thankfully, I am now taking an interest in my life again – gardening, reading, visiting the garden centres, meeting friends and family for coffee. I have now embarked on a hobby which I haven't done for years – crocheting. I have now completed eight beautiful blankets. I am so grateful to have my life back on track and can't emphasise enough how my sister's mindfulness practise has helped all of us to stay focused and be grateful for each day that we live.

Moira D'Agostino

Acknowledgements

Firstly, I would like to thank you, the reader, for taking the time to read my book.

I would like to take this opportunity to thank all the wonderful, motivational and inspirational people who have shared, and continue to share, this mindfulness journey with me: all at Nifty Fifty's, Coatbridge, as well as my mindfulness classes at Larkhall Library and South Lanarkshire College, and my peers and tutors on the MSc in Mindfulness, University of Aberdeen. A special thank you to Robert Grant, tai chi teacher, for all his help and support.

I owe a great deal of gratitude to Martin Stepek, mindfulness teacher, author and poet for introducing me to mindfulness and for his philosophical and compassionate teachings.

A heartfelt thank you to the lovely Ellen Dickie for comforting me when my train, metaphorically speaking, hit the buffers and my life, as I knew it, came to a complete standstill.

Special thanks to my kind and understanding friend, Aileen Murray, for her words of wisdom and guidance.

Sincere gratitude to my soulmate, Pauline Hazelton, for always being there for me during very challenging times.

I would like to also thank Jean Ward for sharing cups of tea, coffee and understanding.

A heartfelt thanks to my dear friend Margaret Robinson for her positive outlook, inspiration and directness.

Special thanks to my lovely friend, Irene McLaughlan, for helping me put the world to rights.

Thanks also to the wonderful Jenifer Strang for just being 'Jenifer'.

A heartfelt hug and gratitude to the lovely Rhona Cunningham for her ongoing kindness, resilience, encouragement and interest in my mindfulness projects which has helped me to find the strength to complete this publication.

I would like to thank my wee dance pal, Myra Stevenson, for her excellent proofreading and editing of this book. Her expert grammatical skills ensured that all dashes, commas and exclamation marks were put in the correct places.

A sincere thank you to Iain Robertson, Lending Voices, South Lanarkshire Libraries for his expertise and professionalism in producing the podcasts for the mindfulness meditations.

A big thank you and hug for my talented nephew, Anthony D'Agostino, for his amazing photography of Bridge of Orchy railway station and Glenfinnan viaduct, depicted on my book cover.

Finally, I would like to thank Grosvenor House Publishing for their efficiency and professionalism in publishing my second book.

Notes

Bonnie – beautiful

Braes – hillside, slope

Doon – the river Doon flows through Ayrshire in Scotland

Fu' – full

Gie – give

Giftie – gift to

Ithers – others

O' – of

Oursels – ourselves

Pow'r – power

Sae – so

Wad – would

Weeble – a brand of children's toys that are roly-poly figures

Ye – you

Bibliography

ARMSTRONG, K., (2011). *Twelve Steps to a Compassionate Life*. London: The Bodley Head.

AZUR, C. M., (2024). *Choosing to invest in your highest self is like unlocking the door to your true potential.* Available: https://www.linkedin.com/posts/cindymarieazur_authenticity-intentionality-beunstoppable-activity-7199378560325705728-1EOT?utm_source=share&utm_medium=member_android [Date Accessed: 26th May 2025].

BLACK, A., (2018). *A Year of Living Mindfully*. London and New York: CICO Books.

BROWN, E., (2010). *Dowsing: The Ultimate Guide for the 21st Century*. London: Hay House UK Ltd.

BURNS, R., (1791). *The Banks O'Doon*.

BURNS, R., (1786). *To A Louse*.

CALM, (2024). *10 biggest red flags in relationships (and what to do about them)* Available: https://blog.calm.com/blog/biggest-red-flags [Date Accessed: 26th May 2025].

CHÖGYAM TRUNGPA RINPOCHE, (2015). *Shambhala: The Sacred Path of the Warrior.* Boston and London: Shambhala Publications.

CHÖJE LAMA YESHE LOSAL RINPOCHE, (2014). *Living Dharma*. Eskdalemuir: Dzalendara Publishing.

CHOPRA, D., (2020). *Total Meditation: Stress Free Living Starts Here.* London: Rider.

DAVIDSON, R.J. and BEGLEY, S., (2013). *The Emotional Life of Your Brain: How to Change the Way You Think, Feel and Live.* London: Hodder and Stoughton Ltd.

DRAPER, B., (2012). *Less is More: Spirituality for Busy Lives.* Oxford: Lion Hudson plc.

DZOGCHEN PONLOP RINPOCHE, (2011). *Rebel Buddha: A Guide to Inner Transformation.* Boston: Shambhala Publications.

EINSTEIN, A., (1879 – 1955). Quote attributed to Einstein.

EURIPIDES, (c. 480 – c. 406 BC). Quote attributed to Euripides.

FAUL, L. and LABAR, K.S., (2023). PubMed: *Mood-congruent Memory Revisited.* Available: https://pubmed.ncbi.nlm.nih.gov/36201828/ [Date Accessed: 26th May 2025].

FRANKL, V. E., (2004). *Man's Search for Meaning: The Classic Tribute to Hope from the Holocaust.* London: Rider.

GERMER, C. K., (2009). *The Mindful Path to Self-Compassion: Freeing Yourself from Destructive Thoughts and Emotions.* New York: The Guilford Press.

GERMER, C.K. and SIEGEL, R.D., (2012). *Wisdom and Compassion in Psychotherapy: Deepening Mindfulness in Clinical Practice.* New York: The Guilford Press.

GIANCOLA, M., PERAZZINI, M., BONTEMPO, D., PERILLI, E. and D'AMICO, S., (2024). Narcissism and Problematic Social Media Use: A Moderated Mediation Analysis of Fear of Missing out and Trait Mindfulness in Youth. *International Journal of Human–Computer Interaction*, 1–11. Available: https://doi.org/10.1080/10447318.2024.2411468 [Date Accessed: 26th May 2025].

GILBERT, P. and CHODEN, (2013). *Mindful Compassion: Using the Power of Mindfulness and Compassion to Transform our Lives.* London: Constable and Robinson Ltd.

KABAT-ZINN, J., (2013). *Full Catastrophe Living: How to Cope with Stress, Pain and Illness using Mindfulness Meditation.* London: Piatkus.

KABAT-ZINN, J., (2017). *Mindfulness for Beginners: Reclaiming the Present Moment – and Your Life.* Mumbai: Jaico Publishing House.

KINSELLA, S., (2003). *Confessions of a Shopaholic.* New York: Dell.

KUKUSHKIN, N. V., CARNEY, R. E., TABASSUM, T. and CAREW, T.J., (2024). New York University. 'Memories are not only in the Brain, new research finds.' *ScienceDaily.* ScienceDaily, 7 November 2024.

NEFF, K., (2015). *Self-Compassion: Stop Beating Yourself Up and Leave Insecurity Behind.* London: Yellow Kite Books, Hodder and Stoughton.

OVID, (1BC). Quote attributed to Ovid.

PETTIE, G., (1576). Quote attributed to Pettie.

RICE, T., ANDERSSON, B. and ULVAEUS, B., (1986). *I Know Him So Well.* Chess the Musical.

ROSENBERG, L. and GUY, D., (1998). *Breath by Breath: The Liberating Practice of Insight Meditation.* Boston: Shambhala Publications.

SEARS, R., (2014). *Mindfulness: Living Through Challenges and Enriching Your Life in This Moment.* Chichester, West Sussex: John Wiley and Sons.

SINCLAIR, M. and SEYDEL, J., (2013). *Mindfulness for Busy People*. Harlow: Pearson Education Limited.

STEPEK, M., (2024). Presentation on his book, Jan Stepek: Gulag to Glasgow (Hamilton, Scotland).

TSOKNYI RINPOCHE and SWANSON, E., (2012). *Open Heart, Open Mind: A Guide to Inner Transformation*. London: Rider.

WAITLEY, D., (1933 – 2025). *Learn from the past, set vivid, detailed goals for the future, and live in the only moment of time over which you have any control: now*. Available: https://www.goodreads.com/quotes/776718-learn-from-the-past-set-vivid-detailed-goals-for-the [Date Accessed: 26th May 2025].

WALLACE, B.A., (2007). *Contemplative Science: Where Buddhism and Neuroscience Converge*. West Sussex: Columbia University Press.

WAX. R., (2018). *How to Be Human: The Manual.* London: Penguin Life.

WEBB, L., (2013). *Resilience: How to cope when everything around you keeps changing*. Chichester: John Wiley and Sons Ltd.

WILLIAMS, M., TEASDALE, J., SEGAL, Z. and KABAT-ZINN, J., (2007). *The Mindful Way Through Depression: Freeing Yourself from Chronic Unhappiness*. New York: The Guilford Press.

YATES, J., IMMERGUT, M. and GRAVES, J., (2017). *The Mind Illuminated.* London: Hay House UK Ltd.

YONGEY MINGYUR RINPOCHE and SWANSON E., (2009). *The Joy of Living.* London: Bantam Books.

About the Author

Eleanor Gibson is a mindfulness practitioner with an MSc in mindfulness which she studied at the University of Aberdeen. She, presently, teaches mindfulness at South Lanarkshire College, Nifty Fifty's in Coatbridge and Larkhall Library. She also gives presentations on mindfulness to community groups in her local area.

Eleanor was born in Motherwell and was educated at Glencairn Primary School, Motherwell; Dalziel High School, Motherwell; The London College of Music; Bell College, Hamilton; Manchester College; University of Strathclyde, Glasgow; City of Glasgow College and the University of Aberdeen.

She is passionate about the benefits of mindfulness in all of our lives and is delighted to share her experiences and learning on the subject through her books *Mindfulness the Journey, Not the Destination* and *Mindfulness – A Different Platform.*

Contact the author at: eleanor@writeme.com

Appendices

Preparation for Formal Mindfulness Practices

- Find a comfortable and peaceful place to sit
- You can have the palms of the hands facing upwards or downwards or just simply place one hand on top of the other with the palms facing upwards, thumbs gently touching and gently resting them on your lap
- You may have the eyes open with a downwards gaze or, if you prefer, you can have the eyes closed
- Always adopt a beginner's mind, as if you have never practised mindfulness before

Appendix A

Mindfulness Practice – RAIN – Also available as a podcast at https://youtube.com/@eleanor-mindfulness

- Sound of bell
- Let's begin our practise by setting a clear intention
- Our intention is to practise mindfulness – present moment awareness, without judgement
- Now be aware of your motivation
- Gently asking yourself, why am I practising mindfulness?
- It may be that you want more clarity in your life, to increase your health and wellbeing or to bring more compassion and kindness into each day
- Now gently checking in with your posture

- Adopting a dignified posture almost like a mountain, making sure that the back is straight
- Really feeling into your posture
- Now be aware of the ground beneath the body and the space surrounding the body
- Be aware of the body breathing
- Gently breathing
- Be aware of the breath as it enters the body at the nostrils and leaves the body through the mouth, breath after breath
- Just gently breathing
- Now breathing a little more deeply than normal and seeing if you can make the inbreath the same length as the outbreath
- Just be with your breathing for the next few moments
- Then when you are ready, focusing more on the outbreath and just seeing if your body can relax a little as you breathe out
- So simply focus gently on the outbreath for a few moments
- Now let your breathing return to its natural rhythm
- Be aware of the weight of the body resting on the ground and the space surrounding the body
- Be aware of sounds moving through space
- Spending a few moments simply resting with sound
- So, your mind is resting on the body, body resting on the ground
- Gently focusing on what you can hear in this moment
- So simply using sound as a support, to anchor you, in this precious moment in time
- Resting with sound for the next few moments
- Then, gently asking yourself how you are feeling in this moment
- What mood, mind state, feeling or strong emotion is present for you right now?
- Simply acknowledge it and where relevant naming it
- Like opening the door to your guest house
- Noticing what it feels like
- Allow the mind state to be there, because it is there, and make it welcome

- It's like asking your guest to have a seat in your guest house
- So simply resting with your guest for a few moments
- Then gently return to sound as your support and what you can hear in this moment
- Allowing your feeling to be present
- Simply resting with sound as your support
- Now gently ask yourself where you are feeling this mind state within the body
- Perhaps a tightness, heat or vibration, maybe at the head, throat, chest or tummy
- Just being aware of where you are experiencing this mood within the body
- Gently returning to sound as your support, the sound of this precious moment in time
- Now, when you are ready, gently ask yourself if the mood or emotion is something that you have become in this moment, or is it just moving through you, like a guest through your guest house
- Opening up around the full experience
- Mind resting on the body, body resting on the ground
- Aware of the space surrounding the body and sounds moving through space
- Simply resting with sound
- Now letting go of your focus on sound and simply resting without focus for a few moments
- Simply resting, until the sound of the bell
- Sound of bell
- Now gently reflect on this practise and ask how you feel right now
- Now gently open your eyes and be accustomed to the light in the room again

Appendix B

Mindfulness Practice – Training the Mind to Focus – Also available as a podcast at https://youtube.com/@eleanor-mindfulness

- Sound of bell
- Begin by setting a very clear intention
- Our intention is to practise mindfulness – present moment awareness, without judgement
- Now be aware of your motivation
- Gently asking yourself, why am I practising mindfulness?
- Now be aware of your posture
- Really feeling into your posture, making sure that the back is straight
- Now simply focus on your breathing
- Gently breathing
- Be aware each time you breathe in and each time you breathe out
- Gently focus on your breathing for the next few moments
- Now taking a few mindful breaths, breathing a little more deeply than normal
- See if you can make the inbreath the same length as the outbreath
- Simply focus on your breathing for the next few moments
- Now focus more on the outbreath and see if your body can relax a little as you breathe out
- Focusing more on the outbreath for the next few moments
- Then let your breathing return to its natural rhythm
- Now be aware of your body sitting here in this room
- Gently move your focus to your right foot, aware of its temperature
- Be aware of how the right foot feels in this moment
- Be aware of any sensations within the right foot
- Giving this part of your body your full attention for the next few moments
- Now gently move your focus to the left hand

- How does the left hand feel in this moment?
- Be aware of the fingertips, fingers, palm of the hand and back of the hand
- Having a felt sense of the left hand and how it actually feels right now
- Giving your left hand your full attention for the next few moments
- Now move your focus to the right knee. How does it feel in this moment?
- Is it warm, cool or just neutral?
- Be aware of any body sensations present for you at the right knee
- Accepting things to be just as they are for the next few moments
- Now gently move your focus to your face
- How does your face feel in this moment?
- What is the temperature like at this part of the body?
- Be aware of your forehead, how does it feel? Relaxed, tense or just neutral?
- Moving your focus to the eyes
- How do the eyes feel in this moment – alert, tired or just neutral?
- Are they moist, dry or just neutral?
- Gently move your focus to the ears
- How do they feel in this moment. Giving the ears your full attention
- Now gently move your focus to the nose
- Perhaps being aware of the breath as it rushes past the nostrils on each inbreath
- Be totally aware of how this feels
- Now moving your focus to the ribcage and be aware of the gentle movement of the ribcage expanding and contracting as you breathe in and out
- Gently breathing
- Simply be with your breathing for the next few moments

- Now gently letting go of your focus on the breath and simply resting without focus for a few moments until the sound of the bell
- Sound of bell
- Now gently reflect on this practise and ask how you feel right now
- Now gently open your eyes and be accustomed to the light in the room again

Appendix C

Mindfulness Practice – Compassionate Image – Also available as a podcast at https://youtube.com/@eleanor-mindfulness

In this meditation, we will bring to mind our ideal compassionate image. This can be a person or animal or perhaps nature itself.

- Sound of bell
- Begin by setting a very clear intention
- Our intention is to practise mindfulness – present moment awareness, without judgement
- Now be aware of your motivation
- Gently asking yourself, why am I practising mindfulness?
- Beginning this practise by settling into your posture
- Adopting a dignified posture
- Now simply be with the soothing rhythm of your breathing, just flowing in and out of the body without force
- So just be with your breathing for the next few moments, no need to force anything
- Now slightly deepening and slowing your breathing and trying to make the inbreath the same length as the outbreath
- Just be with your breathing for the next few moments
- Now focusing a little more on the outbreath and just seeing if your body can relax a little as you breathe out
- Now let your breathing fall back to its natural rhythm and bring your attention more fully into the body
- So just be aware of the weight of the body resting on the ground and be aware of any sensations present within the body
- So gently scanning the body from the crown of the head right down to your toes and reversing the flow from the toes up through the body to the crown of the head again
- Just be aware of any body sensations that are commanding your attention
- Now be aware of the full body and the space surrounding the body

- Now gently let go of any sense of trying to do anything and just simply be
- Allow yourself to experience whatever comes to you through your senses without looking for anything in particular or listening for anything in particular
- You might find after a few moments that your mind starts to wander and that is perfectly okay
- Now letting your focus move to your breathing, allowing your breath to bring you into being fully present
- Gently be with the flow of your breathing, wherever you can connect with it within the body
- Just allowing the breath to be like an anchor, anchoring you in this precious moment in time
- Should the mind wander into thinking mode, just recognise where it's wandered to and return to your breathing
- Now gently bring to mind the qualities of a compassionate image
- A compassionate image with the qualities of kindness, caring and understanding and a sense of belonging
- Your compassionate image wants you to be happy and free from suffering and to flourish with peace and wellbeing
- So simply resting with your compassionate image for the next few moments
- And just being reassured that your compassionate image wants you to be happy, to be at peace and be healthy
- So simply resting with this compassionate image for the next few moments
- Now gently letting your compassionate image gently fade, knowing that you can return to it at any time
- Now simply resting in full awareness for the next few moments until the sound of the bell
- Sound of bell
- Now gently reflect on this practise and ask how you feel right now
- Gently opening your eyes and being accustomed to the light in the room again

Appendix D

Mindfulness Practise - A Safe Place – Also available as a podcast at https://youtube.com/@eleanor-mindfulness

- Sound of bell
- Begin by setting a very clear intention
- Our intention is to practise mindfulness – present moment awareness, without judgement
- Now be aware of your motivation
- Gently asking yourself, why am I practising mindfulness?
- Adopting a dignified posture with the back straight
- Be aware of the ground beneath the body, holding the body unconditionally
- Be aware of the space surrounding the body
- The full body resting on the ground and surrounded by space
- Be aware of the body breathing
- Gently breathing
- Just simply focusing on the breath for the next few moments
- Now taking a few mindful breaths and letting go on the outbreath
- Then when you are ready, allow your breathing to return to its natural rhythm
- As you sit here breathing, allow your imagination to bring a safe place to mind
- A place that makes you feel happy, content and secure
- Now be aware of what you can see in this safe place of yours – colours, shapes and textures
- Resting in awareness of what you can see in your safe place
- Now be aware of the quality of light in this wonderful place of yours
- What time of day is it?
- Simply resting in awareness in your safe place
- Now be aware of what you can hear in your safe place
- What sounds are drifting towards you?
- Simply resting in awareness of what you can hear

- Now be aware of what you can smell in your safe place
- Simply resting in full awareness in this wonderful place
- Now be aware of what you can taste in this place and be aware of whether the mouth is dry, moist or just neutral
- Now be aware of the temperature
- Is it warm, cool or just neutral?
- Now resting in full awareness in your safe place with what you can see, hear, taste and smell, the quality of light and temperature
- Know that this place welcomes you and is happy for you to be there
- Now be aware of how this makes you feel within the body – perhaps a warmth at your heart, lightness in your head, easing of the shoulders
- Simply resting in awareness with all your senses and feelings of being content, secure, welcome and comforted
- Resting in your safe place for as long as is comfortable for you
- Then, when you are ready, stepping back from your safe place knowing that you can return at any time
- Now simply resting without focus for the next few moments until the sound of the bell
- Sound of bell
- Now gently reflect on your practise and gently ask how you are feeling right now
- And gently open your eyes and be accustomed to the light in the room again

Helpful Organisations

AGE SCOTLAND

Helpline **0800 12 44 222**

www.agescotland.org.uk

DOMESTIC ABUSE HELPLINE

The freephone, 24-hour National Domestic Abuse Helpline **0808 2000 247**

https://www.nationaldahelpline.org.uk/

MINDFULNESS ASSOCIATION

info@mindfulnessassociation.net

SAMARITANS

Call **116 123** (free)

https://www.samaritans.org/scotland/how-we-can-help/contact-samaritan/

SUICIDE PREVENTION

Suicide Helpline: Get Help **0800 587 0800**

https://spuk.org.uk/

WOMENS AID

https://www.womensaid.org.uk/

www.ingramcontent.com/pod-product-compliance
Lightning Source LLC
LaVergne TN
LVHW091310080426
835510LV00007B/455
* 9 7 8 1 8 3 6 1 5 4 5 1 8 *